STRASBOURG

Travel Guide

The Ultimate Guide to Strasbourg for First-Timers and Adventurer Seekers, Plus Top Attractions, a 7-Day Well-Planned Itinerary, and Much More

2024

Susanna Clockfield

Strasbourg Travel Guide 2024

The Ultimate Guide to Strasbourg for First-Timers and Adventurer Seekers, Plus Top Attractions, a 7-Day Well-Planned Itinerary, and Much More

Copyright

Table Of Content

Introduction

I was immediately struck by the splendor of Strasbourg as I stepped off the train. The gorgeous architecture, picturesque canals, and busy vitality of the streets all contributed to a sense of excitement and anticipation.

My first trip was the iconic Notre-Dame Cathedral, which towered majestically above the metropolitan skyline. As I entered the cathedral, I was struck by the soaring vaulted ceilings and beautiful stained glass windows that showered the interior in a kaleidoscope of colors.

But it wasn't just the cathedral's majesty that struck me. It was also the calm reverence of the visitors, who went through the sanctuary with wonder and respect for this ancient site of prayer.

After seeing the church, I went to the Petite France area, which is noted for its gorgeous half-timbered houses and picturesque canals. I felt transported back to a bygone era of beautiful European villages as I strolled along the cobblestone alleys.

One of my greatest memories from Strasbourg was discovering a little bakery nestled away on a side street. The aroma of freshly baked bread and pastries wafted out onto the street, luring me inside. I chatted with the nice baker about his skill and his passion for this lovely city while I had a warm croissant and a cup of coffee.

As the day progressed, I proceeded to explore Strasbourg, taking in its numerous sights and noises. From the vibrant flower markets to the boisterous street dancers, there was always something fresh and fascinating around every corner.

But what impressed me the most about Strasbourg was its feeling of history and tradition. Everywhere I went, I felt as if I were following in the footsteps of generations of individuals who had gone before me, each leaving their unique imprint on this lively metropolis.

I felt a bittersweet grief as I boarded the train to depart Strasbourg. But I also knew that the memories and experiences I had gathered throughout my time there would stay with me forever, reminding me of the beauty and charm of this particular city.

- About Strasbourg

Strasbourg, the capital of Alsace in northern France, provides something for everyone. Strasbourg has something for everyone, whether they are interested in history, culture, food, or architecture. Its distinct mix of French and German traditions makes it an enthralling location that draws visitors from all over the world.

The gorgeous architecture in Strasbourg is one of the first things that visitors notice. The city is home to a number of historic structures and attractions, including the well-known Notre-Dame Cathedral. With its soaring vaulted ceilings, complex carvings, and gorgeous stained glass windows, this Gothic masterpiece is one of the most impressive cathedrals in Europe. Visitors can scale the cathedral's tower for sweeping views of the city.

La Petite France, a lovely district with winding canals and charming half-timbered cottages, is another must-see in Strasbourg. This historic region was originally home to tanners, millers, and fisherman, and it is now a popular destination for travelers to walk and take in the sights and sounds. Visitors can also take a boat excursion around the canals to see the city from a new angle.

Strasbourg has a rich and fascinating history for individuals who are interested in history. For centuries, the French and Germans fought over the city, and its distinctive blend of cultures can be seen in its architecture, food, and traditions. The Palais Rohan is an excellent site to begin learning about Strasbourg's history. This 18th-century palace previously housed the city's bishops but is now home to three museums dedicated to art, decorative arts, and archeology.

Another fantastic venue to learn about the region's history and culture is the Alsatian Museum. The museum, which is housed in a 16th-century building, contains displays on traditional Alsatian life, such as clothing, furniture, and crafts. Visitors can also learn about the region's wine-making traditions and try some of the region's wines.

Foodies will enjoy Strasbourg's culinary scene, which combines French and German elements to create a distinctive and delectable cuisine. Tarte flambée, a thin-crust pizza-like dish topped with bacon, onions, and cream, is famous in the city. Traditional Alsatian delicacies such as choucroute (sauerkraut with sausages and potatoes) and baeckeoffe (a stew of pork, potatoes, and vegetables) are also available to visitors.

These foods are best tried at one of Strasbourg's many outdoor markets. There are various markets in the city that provide fresh fruit, meats, cheeses, and baked items. The Christmas market is especially well-known, with stalls selling handcrafted items, ornaments, and delectable snacks like gingerbread and mulled wine.

Strasbourg is also a popular shopping location. The city is home to a mix of high-end boutiques and eccentric local stores selling anything from vintage apparel to handcrafted jewelry. Rue des Grandes Arcades, with its exquisite arcades and premium boutiques, is a popular shopping route.

- When to Visit

To make the most of this wonderful site, arrive at the correct time. Whether you're fascinated by the wintry wonderland of Christmas markets or the vivid colors of spring, each season in Strasbourg has its own distinct appeal.

Spring is from March until May.

Strasbourg transforms into a magnificent wonderland as the winter chill gives way to the warmth of spring. The gardens of the city come alive with brilliant blooms, and the good weather promotes leisurely strolls along La Petite France's lovely canals. Spring is a great time to visit if you want to avoid the crowds and enjoy the beauty of nature in bloom.

The homecoming of the storks is one of the highlights of spring in Strasbourg. These beautiful birds, considered good luck symbols, nest all over the city. It's a genuinely amazing experience to witness them against the backdrop of blossoming trees. In addition, spring heralds the start of the outdoor festival season, which includes events celebrating music, art, and gastronomy. The squares and parks of the city are transformed into venues for vibrant performances and cultural festivals.

Summer runs from June until August.

The energy in Strasbourg rises as the temperature rises. Summertime in the city has a joyous vibe, with longer days allowing for more exploration. Strasbourg Cathedral rises boldly, and the streets are bustling with a mix of inhabitants and tourists. Summer is ideal for savoring the city's renowned culinary scene at outdoor cafes or taking a leisurely boat ride along the Ill River.

The Strasbourg Music Festival, which turns the city into a platform for classical and contemporary music, is unquestionably the summer highlight in Strasbourg. The sunny evenings are also great for exploring the city's nightlife, with a variety of bars and clubs giving a bustling environment. Summer is the ideal time to visit Strasbourg for anyone looking for a mix of cultural events and exciting street life.

Autumn runs from September to November.

Strasbourg takes on a charming and cozy atmosphere when the leaves change hues. Autumn is a calmer season, making it ideal for contemplative walks in the city's parks, such as the Orangerie Park or the Robertsau Forest. The October colors complement the old architecture and create a stunning setting.

The beginning of the harvest season occurs in September, and the city celebrates with wine festivals and gourmet activities. Tourists can savor the region's delectable wines and traditional Alsatian delicacies, immersing themselves in the region's rich gastronomy. Various cultural events and exhibitions are also held throughout the fall season, giving guests a more intimate and relaxed experience.

Winter runs from December until February.

During the winter, Strasbourg is transformed into a fairy-tale setting, giving it the moniker "Capital of Christmas." The city's Christmas markets, which date back to 1570, are a must-see spectacle. As the city shines with lights and decorations, the aroma of mulled wine and freshly cooked gingerbread fills the air.

Millions of visitors from all over the world flock to the Strasbourg Christmas market, which is located around the Cathedral and in La Petite, France. The Grande Île, a UNESCO World Heritage site, is decked out in holiday lights, offering a lovely setting for a winter vacation. Winter in Strasbourg provides a unique opportunity to immerse oneself in the warmth of the holiday spirit while experiencing the city's rich traditions.

- Getting Around

Buses in Strasbourg

Navigating the city's streets via the large bus network is not only practical, but also an adventure waiting to happen.

Strasbourg Bus Symphony:

As you walk through Strasbourg's bustling streets, the city's public bus system reveals itself as a symphonic symphony, delivering a melodious tour through its charming sections. The buses, which are seamlessly incorporated into the fabric of the city, serve as your ticket to the hidden gems that lie beyond the postcard-perfect scenes.

The Bus Line Ballet:

Strasbourg's bus system is a finely organized ballet of lines, each of which takes you on a different route across the city's numerous neighborhoods. Whether you're drawn to the historical elegance of La Petite France or the sophistication of the European Quarter, a bus route will take you there.

CTS - The Ballet Masters:

The maestros of transportation, Compagnie des Transports Strasbourgeois (CTS), are at the core of this ballet. This public transportation organization coordinates the movements of buses, trams, and even boats, ensuring that tourists visiting Strasbourg have a flawless experience. The buses are more than just transportation; they are performers in a huge performance that will make your journey as exciting as the destinations themselves.

The Overture - Route Planning:

Begin your Strasbourg experience by purchasing a Strasbourg Pass, which will provide you access to the city's public transit. You can use the pass to access a vast network of buses, trams, and even Batorama boat trips. The pass not only makes your journey easier, but it also adds a magical touch to your tour of Strasbourg.

Act I: The Importance of Place Kléber:

The city's pulsing heart, Place Kléber, serves as the stage for various bus acts. Diverse lines intersect here, providing access to numerous districts. Imagine yourself as an audience member, excitedly anticipating the emerging splendor of Strasbourg's surroundings as you board a bus.

Act II: Buses as Narrators:

Every bus trip in Strasbourg tells a different story, offering an insight into the city's rich history as well as modern life. Consider yourself on Bus Line 10, traveling through La Petite France's cobblestone streets. The bus takes on the role of narrator, telling stories about half-timbered mansions and flower-filled balconies.

Act III - Line 6:

Line 6 emerges as the dominant character for those looking for a grandiose experience. This bus takes a panoramic tour of the European Quarter and the stately Council of Europe. In a matter of minutes, the bus transforms into a time machine, bringing you from the medieval to the futuristic.

The Riverside Romance:

A crescendo builds along the riverbanks as the busses negotiate the streets of Strasbourg. Line 30, in particular, orchestrates a riverbank romance, with stunning views of the Rhine. Imagine sitting at a window, watching the river flow through the city, casting reflections on centuries-old buildings.

Interlude - Strasbourg Melody:

Take a break between bus rides to listen to the Strasbourg melody. Stop by one of the beautiful cafés that line the streets, where the perfume of freshly made pastries blends with the calm hum of the city. Allow Strasbourg's rhythm to permeate your spirit before the next act begins.

The Bus-Boat Encore:

Enjoy the bus-boat encore to round up your musical adventure. Board Bus Line 21, which converts into a boat and allows you to sail through Strasbourg's waterways. This conclusion exemplifies the city's adaptability, with busses transformed into boats and the journey as lovely as the destination.

The buses are the characters in the magnificent tapestry of Strasbourg's attraction, weaving together the threads of history, culture, and modernity. Embrace the city's rhythm, let the buses be your guides, and let Strasbourg's enthralling story develop with each stop and turn.

Walking and bicycling

Walking and bicycling are excellent ways to discover the city's charms because they provide an intimate and immersive experience that reveals the city's beauty at a leisurely pace.

Strasbourg walking tour:

Step into the heart of Strasbourg's historic district, Grande Île, a UNESCO World Heritage site, and embark on an enthralling journey through narrow cobblestone streets. Begin your exploration at the iconic Strasbourg Cathedral, a Gothic architectural masterpiece. The intricate facade of the cathedral and its towering spire serve as a magnificent starting point for your walking adventure.

You'll find timber-framed houses adorned with colorful flowers as you meander through the quaint lanes, each telling a story from centuries ago. With its half-timbered houses reflected in the calm waters of the Ill River, the district of La Petite France adds a fairytale-like quality to your stroll. Immerse yourself in the charm of this charming neighborhood, which is known for its artisan shops, cafes, and the enchanting Covered Bridges.

Visit the Strasbourg Historical Museum, which is housed in a 16th-century building, for a cultural break. Discover Strasbourg's rich history through fascinating exhibits, including artifacts that trace the city's evolution from medieval times to the present.

A stroll along the canals is essential to any exploration of Strasbourg. The Ill River runs through the city, providing scenic views as well as the opportunity to admire the medieval architecture that lines its banks. Cross charming bridges adorned with turrets like Ponts Couverts to experience the timeless beauty of this European gem.

Bicycling Excursions:

Get on a bike and explore Strasbourg's extensive network of bike paths to cover more ground and see the city from a different perspective. The city is well-known for its dedication to cycling, with dedicated lanes making it easy and safe for visitors to pedal through the enchanting streets.

Begin your cycling adventure by renting a bike from one of the city's many rental stations. Cruise along the Rhine River on dedicated bike paths that offer breathtaking views of the water and surrounding landscape. The flat terrain of Strasbourg makes it accessible to cyclists of all levels, ensuring an enjoyable ride for all.

Visit the Parc de l'Orangerie for a breath of fresh air and a taste of nature. This sprawling park, which dates back to the 17th century, provides a tranquil setting for cyclists. Pedal beneath the lush canopy of trees, explore the French and English gardens, and enjoy the peace and quiet of this urban oasis.

A cycling trip would be incomplete unless you explored the extensive network of bike paths that connect Strasbourg to the charming villages and vineyards of the Alsace region. Travel through the vineyards, stopping at local wineries to sample the region's well-known wines. The picturesque landscapes and charming villages provide a welcome diversion from the urban allure of Strasbourg.

Culinary Highlights:

Walking and biking in Strasbourg are both excellent ways to sample the city's culinary offerings. Stop for a flaky croissant or a classic Alsatian dish like tarte flambée, a thin pizza-like creation topped with cream, onions, and bacon.

Discover hidden gems like the markets where locals gather to showcase fresh produce, cheeses, and artisanal products as you explore the various neighborhoods. Strasbourg's food scene is a delectable blend of French and German influences, providing a culinary adventure to complement the city's cultural tapestry.

Finally, walking and bicycling in Strasbourg provide access to the city's treasures that no other mode of transportation can. Whether you choose to walk through its historic streets or ride along its scenic bike paths, every step and turn of the wheel reveals the magic of Strasbourg—a city that seamlessly blends history, culture, and natural beauty into an unforgettable experience for every tourist.

My Personal Experience

As the sun rose over Strasbourg's cobblestone streets, I found myself in the shadow of the magnificent Strasbourg Cathedral. Eager to immerse myself in the allure of Strasbourg, I decided to embark on a day of exploration, opting for the time-honored combination of walking and bicycling to weave through the tapestry of the city's charm.

Morning Walk:

As I drove through the narrow lanes of Grande Île, the air was crisp. The Strasbourg Cathedral towered above me, its ornate facade capturing my attention. Each step took me deeper into the old town, where timber-framed houses adorned with vibrant flowers whispered stories of centuries gone by.

The enchantment grew as I approached La Petite, France. The calm waters of the Ill River reflected half-timbered houses, creating a scene straight out of a storybook. Outdoor cafes beckoned, and the aroma of freshly baked pastries filled the air. It was a sensory overload, a symphony of sights, sounds, and smells that captured the essence of Strasbourg.

Interlude Cultural:

I went to the Strasbourg Historical Museum, eager to learn about the city's history. The museum, housed in a 16th-century structure, told the story of the city through artifacts and exhibits. The museum provided a captivating journey through time, from medieval artifacts to glimpses of Strasbourg's evolution.

As I continued my walk along the canals, the sun reached its zenith, and I passed through picturesque bridges adorned with flowers. The turrets and medieval charm of Ponts Couverts attested to the city's timeless beauty. The Ill River's soothing rhythm accompanied me, providing a peaceful backdrop to my exploration.

Pedaling Throughout the Day:

I decided to transition to bicycling after a leisurely lunch at a riverside cafe for a broader perspective. I rented a bike from a nearby station and pedaled along the Rhine River, the wind in my hair whispering. The journey was made easier by dedicated bike paths, and the city's commitment to cycling was evident with every turn of the wheel.

The Parc de l'Orangerie arose as a green oasis, providing a welcome respite from the cityscape. I cycled through the French and English gardens, the scent of blooming flowers in the air. The park was a tranquil haven in the midst of the city, a hidden gem just waiting to be discovered.

Culinary Delights and Vineyards

After leaving the city limits, I took the bike paths that led to the Alsace vineyards. The undulating landscapes unfolded, and on the horizon, quaint villages appeared. I tasted the region's renowned wines at local wineries, each sip a celebration of the terroir that defines Alsace.

The drive back to Strasbourg took me through picturesque villages where time seemed to stand still. I ate flaky croissants, savory tarte flambée, and experienced the warmth of local hospitality along the way. The markets provided a glimpse into daily life, with locals gathering to showcase the region's bounty.

As the sun set below the horizon, casting a warm glow over Strasbourg, I realized that my day of walking and bicycling had been more than just an exploration; it had been a journey through a city's soul. Strasbourg's streets, canals, and parks had become chapters in a personal story, with each step and pedal stroke instilling memories that would linger long after the journey was over.

Taxis and rideshares

Navigating the city with taxis and ride-sharing services is not just a means of getting from point A to point B; it's an immersive experience that enhances the overall visit.

Taxis in Strasbourg:

Taxis in Strasbourg are a reliable and comfortable mode of transportation for tourists eager to explore the city without the hassle of navigating public transportation. The iconic white taxis with their distinctive blue signs are a common sight throughout the city, offering a seamless blend of traditional service with modern convenience.

One of the notable features of Strasbourg's taxi service is the high level of professionalism and courtesy exhibited by the drivers. Fluent in English and often other languages, these drivers serve as friendly ambassadors, ready to provide tourists with not just a ride, but also valuable insights into the city's history and culture. Whether you're seeking recommendations for local cuisine or tips on the best time to visit popular attractions, Strasbourg's taxi drivers are an invaluable source of information.

In terms of accessibility, taxis are readily available at designated taxi stands, major transportation hubs, and can also be hailed on the street. For those who prefer the convenience of modern technology, various taxi-hailing apps make it easy to summon a cab with just a few taps on a smartphone. This blend of traditional service and technological innovation ensures that visitors have multiple options to suit their preferences.

Ride-Sharing Services:

Complementing the traditional taxi experience in Strasbourg are ride-sharing services, which have gained popularity for their affordability and user-friendly interfaces. International visitors familiar with popular ride-sharing apps will find comfort in the seamless transition to services like Uber and Lyft, which operate in Strasbourg.

The ride-sharing experience in Strasbourg not only provides a convenient way to explore the city but also offers a unique opportunity to engage with locals. Conversations with drivers often reveal hidden gems and off-the-beaten-path attractions that might not be found in guidebooks. The personal touch of these interactions adds a layer of authenticity to the tourist experience, turning a simple ride into a memorable cultural exchange.

Beyond the convenience of hailing a ride with a few taps on a smartphone, ride-sharing services contribute to the city's commitment to sustainability. As Strasbourg strives to be a more eco-friendly destination, ride-sharing offers an environmentally conscious option for tourists looking to reduce their carbon footprint while enjoying the city.

Exploring Strasbourg:

Both taxis and ride-sharing services play a crucial role in enhancing the tourist experience in Strasbourg. The city's well-planned infrastructure, combined with the warmth of its people, ensures that every journey is an opportunity to discover something new. Whether it's a leisurely ride along the Rhine

River or a quick transfer to the historic district of La Petite France, taxis and ride-sharing services seamlessly connect tourists to the heart of Strasbourg's vibrant culture.

Visa Requirements

As I stepped off the train in Strasbourg, the buttery aroma of warm pretzels mixed with the crisp December air tickled my nose. The medieval rooftops were dusted with snow, giving the cobblestone streets a fairytale sparkle. For years, Susanna, an impulsive travel guide book Writer with a chronic case of wanderlust, had wished to visit this Alsatian treasure. I'd booked my ticket on a whim, armed with a Canon and a desire for Christmas markets, oblivious to the bureaucratic stumbling block that awaited.

Imagine my surprise when, with my passport in hand, I was greeted with a furrowed brow and the terse, "Vous avez un visa?" My French sputtered into panicked gibberish, rusty from high school classes. My American passport, which is valid throughout the Schengen zone (except for Strasbourg), was apparently insufficient for a festive frolic in this border town. Dreams of sipping vin chaud in front of the cathedral and nibbling on pain d'épices cookies vanished like wisps of chimney smoke.

I trudged out of the station, visions of gingerbread houses and twinkling lights replaced by the looming prospect of spending Christmas Eve in a sterile airport hotel. But then, in the midst of the swirling snowflakes, a ray of hope appeared: a cozy cafe smelling enticingly of freshly baked croissants. I poured out my woes to the kind barista, Madame Claire, seeking solace in coffee and carbs.

Claire assured me, with a twinkle in her eye and a smattering of French, "Strasbourg ne laissera pas une aventurière comme toi partir les mains vides!" (Strasbourg will not let you leave empty-handed!). So began my unexpected visa odyssey, a whirlwind of wrong turns, chance meetings, and a crash course in French bureaucracy.

Claire took on the role of my fairy godmother, guiding me through the maze of officialdom. We went to the Prefecture, a grand stone structure that resembled a medieval castle rather than a government office. Claire patiently deciphered my hieroglyphics and offered pep talks between stamps and signatures while I filled out forms in broken French.

The procedure was far from straightforward. There were dead ends and moments when visas seemed as elusive as Santa's elves. But each obstacle cleared brought a rush of adrenaline, and all the while, Strasbourg worked its magic. The aroma of mulled wine warmed my cheeks as I strolled through the Petite France district, half-timbered houses festooned with Christmas lights. I discovered hidden courtyards with nativity scenes, and the majestic Christmas tree in the Grand Place sparkled like a celestial beacon.

Despite my mangled French, the locals were consistently helpful. An elderly couple shared their homemade Alsatian plum cake with me, shopkeepers patiently answered my innumerable questions, and a group of students even invited me to join them in their Christmas Eve caroling. Strasbourg gradually became more than a location; it became a feeling, a tapestry woven with kindness, resilience, and a shared love of holiday cheer.

Finally, on Christmas Eve morning, a small green stamp appeared in my passport, granting me access to the Schengen wonderland. I dashed back to the Grand Place, my eyes welling up with tears of joy (and relief). The Christmas market, which had once been a mirage, was now a tangible feast for the senses, the air thick with the scent of cinnamon and spices, and the stalls brimming with handcrafted ornaments and delectable treats.

I sipped vin chaud beneath the cathedral's spires on Christmas Eve, the twinkling lights reflecting the stars in my eyes. Strasbourg, which had met me with a closed door at first, had opened its arms wide, offering an adventure far richer than any planned itinerary. Instead of being a detour, my visa snafu led me deeper into the heart of the city and its people.

So, dear reader, embrace the unexpected if you find yourself stumbling through Strasbourg, visa problems or not. With its cobblestone streets and Christmas magic, this charming city has a way of weaving its own serendipitous threads into your travel tapestry. And who knows, your own visa saga may turn out to be the most treasured souvenir of all.

Now for the details!

Remember, my story is only a glimpse into the world of visa requirements in Strasbourg. Here's a step-by-step guide to making your trip enjoyable and festive:

Types of Visas:

Short-stay visa (Schengen) valid for up to 90 days: The most common visa for tourists from countries other than the Schengen zone (including the United States).
Long-stay visa: Required for stays of more than 90 days within 180 days.

Required Documents:

Passport must be valid for at least three months after your planned departure from the Schengen zone.
visa completed

Chapter 1: 7 Best Top Attractions

Strasbourg, in the Alsace region of northern France, is a city where cobblestone alleys whisper tales of bygone periods and half-timbered buildings filled with flower boxes burst with colorful life. It's a location where French elegance waltzes with Germanic zeal, producing a cultural tapestry as rich and intricate as the stained glass windows of its famed cathedral. So, put on your walking shoes, grab your beret (optional, but encouraged!), and join us on a journey around the 7 best top attractions that will captivate you with Strasbourg's beauty.

1. Cathédrale Notre-Dame: Prepare to be astounded by Strasbourg's crown treasure, the Cathédrale Notre-Dame. This Gothic masterpiece, decorated with gargoyles and piercing spires, has stood watch for nearly eight centuries. Step inside to be enveloped in the ethereal glow of stained glass windows, each a kaleidoscope of biblical stories and bright hues. Don't miss the astronomical clock, a mechanical marvel that performs a daily puppet play at noon depicting the cosmos and the passage of time. Climb the 332 steps to the platform for stunning views of the city and the Rhine River, a scene that will stay with you forever.

2. La Petite France: Imagine canals lined with half-timbered cottages painted in pastel hues, bridges covered with flowers, and the soft sound of water lapping against stone. Welcome to La Petite France, Strasbourg's most charming area. Stroll around the Quai des Bateliers, take in the wonderful atmosphere, and perhaps indulge in a slice of indulgent tarte flambée, a local flatbread topped with onion and bacon, at one of the small cafes. Rent a paddleboat and cruise the canals, feeling as if you've stumbled into a storybook. In the evening, see the bridges light up, transforming the area into a glittering fantasy.

3. Palais Rohan: For a taste of grandeur, visit the Palais Rohan, a former bishop's palace that now contains three museums: the Museum of Fine Arts, the Archaeological Museum, and the Decorative Arts Museum. Wander through luxurious rooms decorated with tapestries and gilded ceilings, marvel at ancient Roman antiquities, and lose yourself in the grandeur of paintings by masters such as Monet and Rubens. Each museum provides a unique glimpse into Strasbourg's rich history and creative heritage, guaranteeing that there is something to pique everyone's attention.

4. Barrage Vauban: Escape the city center and discover peace at the Barrage Vauban, a 17th-century dam created by the famed military engineer Vauban. Rent a bike and cycle along the scenic trail that follows the Ill River, taking in the lush vegetation and the soft air. Stop near the dam and take in the serene beauty of the river falling over the stones. Pack a picnic basket and locate a peaceful location on the grassy banks to let nature's serenity wash over you.

5. Neustadt (New Town): Step back in time to the nineteenth century in the Neustadt area, a testimony to German dominance at the time. Wide avenues lined with exquisite houses in neo-classical and Wilhelminian styles provide a dramatic contrast to the medieval charm of the old town. Stroll around the lush squares, observe the elegant facades, and perhaps indulge in little retail therapy at the Galeries Lafayette, a big department store located in a spectacular Art Nouveau edifice.

6. Petite Venise: Want to get a taste of Venice without leaving France? Visit Petite Venise, a lovely canal neighborhood in Neustadt. Quaint bridges spanned over small rivers, colorful barges bobbing gently, and flower-bedecked balconies create a touch of Italian beauty within Strasbourg. Sip a coffee at a waterfront cafe, watch boats pass by, and let your mind transport you to Venice's canals.

7. Christmas Markets: If you're lucky enough to visit Strasbourg during the holiday season, prepare to be wowed by its renowned Christmas markets. The entire city is transformed into a winter wonderland of dazzling lights, wooden kiosks brimming with homemade ornaments and delectable snacks, and the air is filled with the aroma of mulled wine and gingerbread. Wander through the several markets, each with its own distinct atmosphere, and drink up the infectious holiday mood. Enjoy live music, sample local specialties, and locate the ideal gifts for your loved ones.

Strasbourg is a city that wants to be explored, relished, and experienced. This Alsatian jewel has something for everyone, from its stately cathedral to its lovely canals, from its rich history to its vibrant festive atmosphere. So pack your luggage, put on your walking shoes, and let Strasbourg work its charm on you.

Take a boat cruise on the Ill River for a very unique experience. Glide past famous sites, appreciate the city from a new perspective, and learn about Strasbourg's interesting history.

Getting to These Places

Strasbourg's small size and good public transit system make it a tourist's dream. Whether you like to stroll, cycle, or use the tram, getting around is a breeze, enabling you to focus on taking in the city's magic.

Here's a rundown of your transit options:

Walking is the greatest way to properly appreciate Strasbourg's small atmosphere. Most central landmarks, such as the Petite France and the Cathedral, are within walking distance of one another, allowing you to discover hidden jewels and lovely alleys along the route. Comfortable shoes are essential, and don't forget to arrange your route around bridge crossings.

Cycling: Strasbourg is a cycling heaven! Exploring on two wheels is both enjoyable and efficient, thanks to dedicated lanes and a plethora of rental businesses. Rent a bike at the train station or in the city center and cycle along the lovely canals, through lush parks, and past historical landmarks. Just remember to obey traffic laws and be cautious of pedestrians.

Public Transportation: Strasbourg's tram network is clean, efficient, and covers the majority of the city. Tickets are inexpensive and simple to obtain from machines located at tram stops. The bus network is a suitable choice for longer journeys or out-of-the-way sights such as the Barrage Vauban. Remember to validate your ticket after you've boarded.

Taxis are widely available in major squares and stands across the city. While convenient, they are the most expensive mode of transportation.

If you take a cab, be sure the meter is turned on to avoid any unpleasant surprises.

Boat Tours: For a fresh perspective, enjoy a boat excursion on the Ill River. Several firms provide varied tours that let you to glide by historical sites, see the city from a watery vantage point, and learn about Strasbourg's intriguing history.

Here are some other recommendations for navigating around Strasbourg:

Purchase a Strasbourg Pass for cheap admission to museums and sites, unlimited public transportation, and even boat cruises. Download the "Strasbourg City Guide" app for maps, walking routes, and real-time public transportation information.

Don't be scared to ask locals for directions. The majority of Strasbourg inhabitants are polite and willing to assist.

Getting around Strasbourg is a lovely experience, regardless of your preferred form of transportation. So, enjoy the city's walkability, get on a tram, or rent a bike, and let Strasbourg reveal its charm at your own leisure.

Bonus Tip: Rent a Vélo'stras, the city's bike-sharing program, for a really local experience. With stations conveniently positioned around the city, it's a cheap and flexible way to experience Strasbourg like a genuine Alsatian.

Chapter 2: Neighborhoods to Explore

A city with cobblestone streets that whisper Hansel and Gretel stories, half-timbered buildings that gleam with Christmas happiness, and the Ill River that twirls like a silver ribbon through a mythical country. But, beyond the postcard-perfect front, Strasbourg's character appears through its numerous neighborhoods, each of which is a hidden gem waiting to be discovered. So, fellow adventurer, put on your walking shoes and let's explore 10 of the city's most interesting corners:

1. La Petite France: Dive deeply into the pulsing heart of Strasbourg. Canals here serenade centuries-old buildings covered with flower boxes, with their vibrant reflections dancing on the water. Alsatian treats like flammekueche (savory flatbread) and kougelhopf (sweet brioche) lure you into charming cafes that spill onto cobblestone pathways. Get lost in the maze of Rue du Brochet, a former tanners' area, and emerge at Ponts Couverts, a line of covered bridges that whispers secrets from the past.

2. La Grande-Île: Stepping into this UNESCO World Heritage Site is like stepping into a Renaissance fantasy. Notre Dame Cathedral, with its stained-glass windows bursting with biblical stories, dominates the skyline. Wander through the Petite Venise, where canals wind through pastel-colored residences, and cross over Pont Rohan, which is ornamented with playful gargoyles that keep watch over the city. Don't miss Kammerzell House, an architectural marvel embellished with oriels and wood sculptures, with an Alsatian whimsical exterior.

3. Neustadt: Cross the river and travel back in time to Prussia. This region is distinguished by wide avenues lined with chestnut trees and stately buildings with exquisite balconies. Climb the Barrage Vauban, a former dam with panoramic vistas, and then stroll through the

lush Parc de l'Orangerie, where swans serenade lovers on pedal boats. Visit the Museum of Modern and Contemporary Art for a taste of the avant-garde, where bold displays will test your preconceptions.

4. Petite Venise: Allow your gondola to act as your imagination as you drift through this small Venice, where waterways reflect half-timbered cottages blooming with geraniums. Pont Saint-Martin, with its Renaissance waterwheel, is a photographer's dream, while Rue des Moulins, with its lovely watermills, speaks of a bygone period. Stop for a coffee and a slice of tarte flambée at a canal-side cafe and listen to the calm murmur of the water as you watch the world float by.

5. Quartier Européen: In this cosmopolitan quarter, you can feel the pulse of European

togetherness. The European Parliament and Council of Europe are housed in sleek modern structures that stand in stark contrast to the historic core. Immerse yourself in the multilingual buzz of cafes and restaurants before seeing the Parlamentarium, an interactive museum that tells the story of Europe through multimedia exhibits.

6. Gare-Tribunal: In this trendy neighborhood, gritty meets chic. Street art adorns brick walls, contemporary boutiques coexist with vintage shops, and busy bars pour out onto lively plazas. Local producers lure you with artisanal cheeses, fresh produce, and Alsatian wines in the covered Marché Gare. Attend a concert at La Laiterie, a renovated dairy factory humming with alternative vibes, in the evening.

7. Krutenau: This island retreat is reminiscent of a hidden garden within the city. The charming canals adorned with weeping willows and colorful houseboats tell stories of bohemian souls. Discover the hidden riches of the Marché aux Poissons, a lively fish market where sea creatures glitter like pearls, after exploring the covered bridges, each a unique link to the past. Later, picnic on the Ill's banks and watch the sky light up with city lights.

8. Bourse-Esplanade: A green oasis in the center of the metropolis. The enormous Parc de l'Étoile shines with manicured lawns, sculptures hidden among the trees, and a tiny train chugging around a lake. Explore the opulent Palais Rohan, a former bishop's residence, before marveling at the exquisite astronomical clock located within the Cathédrale Saint-Thomas. Sip a drink of

Riesling at a cafe on Place Gutenberg as twilight illuminates the sky.

9. Neudorf: This bustling quarter embodies Strasbourg's multicultural soul. Mosques and Buddhist temples coexist with ancient Alsatian structures, creating a religious and ethnic tapestry. Try Vietnamese pho or Moroccan tagines before exploring the Marché Neudorf's labyrinthine alleys, where spices fill the air and treasures await discovery. In the evening, visit Cinéma Le Star for a Bollywood film or a Senegalese concert, your passport to a world beyond borders.

How to Make Friends with the Locals

In this guide, we reveal the keys of building long-lasting connections with the locals, ensuring that your stay is more than just a tour but a genuine cultural immersion.

1. Learn Basic French Phrases: Learn a few important French phrases to start meaningful conversations. Locals appreciate the effort, and it instantly bridges the communication gap, creating a warm and friendly atmosphere.

2. Visit Neighborhood marketplaces: Dive into Strasbourg's daily life by visiting its lively marketplaces. Engage with sellers, eat local delicacies, and strike up a discussion. The marketplaces provide a vibrant environment in which contacts organically flourish.

3. Attend Local Events and Festivals: Immerse yourself in Strasbourg's rich cultural tapestry by visiting events and festivals. Whether it's the renowned Strasbourg Christmas Market or a local music festival, these gatherings provide a unique opportunity to mingle with inhabitants in a festive and relaxed setting.

4. Join Social Media Groups: Connect with locals online through social media channels. Join local clubs or forums where residents share insights and advice and frequently plan meet-ups. This digital strategy might help you connect before and throughout your stay.

5. Attend Workshops and Classes: Attending workshops or classes allows you to discover common interests. Whether it's a cooking lesson, an art workshop, or a language course,

these activities foster relationships with both residents and fellow travelers.

6. Volunteer for Community Projects: Give back to the community by volunteering for local initiatives. This not only allows you to positively contribute, but it also introduces you to like-minded folks who share a passion for making a difference.

7. Participate in Outdoor Activities: Strasbourg's stunning landscapes provide an ideal setting for outdoor activities. Join group tours, hiking clubs, or cycling excursions to meet locals who share your passion for nature and adventure.

8. Stop into local cafés and pubs to strike up a discussion. The easygoing atmosphere is ideal for connecting with locals over a cup of coffee

or a glass of regional wine. Don't be scared to strike up a discussion; the locals are generally eager to share their experiences and advice.

9. Respect Local Customs and Traditions: Show cultural sensitivity by honoring local customs and traditions. This not only creates friendliness but also demonstrates your genuine desire in embracing the local way of life.

Top 10 Public Figure in Strasbourg

Let us delve into the fascinating world of Strasbourg's top ten public people, learning about their lives and the impact they've had on this charming city.

Mayor Roland Ries is the charismatic leader at the helm of Strasbourg's municipal affairs, noted for his progressive ideas and strong commitment to the city's prosperity. During his tenure, tremendous progress has been made in infrastructure, sustainable urban planning, and cultural activities, making him a popular figure in Strasbourg.

Alain Lamassoure, a member of Europarl:

Alain Lamassoure, a mainstay in European politics, represents Strasbourg with distinction in the European Parliament. His ardent commitment for cross-border collaboration and economic development has positioned him as a vital player on the European arena, creating international links that benefit the entire continent, not only Strasbourg.

Renowned Chef Étienne Klein: Chef Étienne Klein's creative approach to Alsatian cuisine has won global acclaim. Chef Klein has become a culinary ambassador for Strasbourg, attracting food fans from all over the world to relish his wonderful dishes.

Human Rights Campaigner Anne-Sophie Pelletier is a French actress.
Anne-Sophie Pelletier, a human rights activist, has devoted her life to fighting social

inequalities in Strasbourg and beyond. Her work as the creator of a prominent local NGO has raised awareness about issues such as homelessness and prejudice, spawning a wave of grassroots activism that continues to benefit the community.

Historian Professor Marie Leclerc: Professor Marie Leclerc is a knowledge beacon in Strasbourg, known for her innovative studies into the city's history. Her engaging lectures and publications have not only benefited the academic community, but have also rekindled local interest in understanding and maintaining Strasbourg's unique historical tapestry.

Camille Durand, an established artist whose works fill galleries and public settings, is a muse for Strasbourg's thriving art scene. Durand's evocative works, which are frequently inspired by Strasbourg's distinctive blend of heritage and modernity, serve as a visual narrative that captivates both inhabitants and visitors, bringing a splash of color to the city's cultural scene.

Environmental activist François Dubois emerges as a key player in Strasbourg's eco-conscious movement in an era when environmental issues take center stage. Many people regard him as a driving force behind the city's commitment to a greener future because of his relentless efforts to promote sustainability, lower carbon footprints, and increase green spaces.

Isabelle Martin, a creative businesswoman, has played a critical role in defining Strasbourg's business scene. She exemplifies the spirit of innovation and economic growth as the founder of a successful tech startup, adding to the city's image as a hub for cutting-edge industries and creating a culture of entrepreneurship.

Literary Star Thierry Dubois: The presence of Thierry Dubois, a prolific novelist whose works frequently take inspiration from the city's wonderful ambiance, enhances Strasbourg's literary landscape. His novels, short tales, and essays strike a chord with readers, taking them on a literary tour through Strasbourg's streets and lanes, leaving a literary legacy that embodies the city's essence.

Fatima Khoury is a grassroots community organizer whose commitment to creating unity and inclusivity has left an indelible mark. She draws individuals from different backgrounds together through her activities, providing a sense of belonging and solidarity that enriches Strasbourg's social fabric.

Traditional Strasbourg Cuisine

Get ready to tantalize your taste buds with the flavors of Traditional Strasbourg Cuisine as you embark on a gastronomic journey through this charming city.

1. Alsatian Flavors: Traditional Strasbourg Cuisine is a delectable fusion of French and German influences, a testament to the region's complicated history. The Alsatian palate is distinguished by a harmonious blend of rich, hearty flavors that highlight the abundance of local produce and a deep respect for culinary traditions.

2. Alsatian Classics: Begin your culinary adventure with timeless Alsatian classics. Tarte flambée, also known as Flammekueche in the

Netherlands, is a thin-crust pizza-style dish topped with crème fraîche, onions, and bacon. Crispy, golden edges combine with creamy toppings to create a symphony of textures and flavors.

3. Charming Winstubs: Step into a Winstub, a cozy Alsatian tavern, to truly immerse yourself in traditional Strasbourg cuisine. These establishments exude warmth and authenticity, and they make ideal settings for sampling regional specialties. Order a potée alsacienne, a hearty pot roast stew brimming with sausages, cabbage, and root vegetables - a warm dish that reflects the region's rustic charm.

4. Culinary Alchemy: Investigate the culinary alchemy of Alsatian chefs as they transform everyday ingredients into culinary masterpieces. The essence of this gastronomic

magic is captured in Baeckeoffe, a slow-cooked casserole of marinated meats, potatoes, and aromatic spices. The result is a flavor explosion that will leave you wanting more.

5. Charming Markets and Fresh Produce: Visit one of Strasbourg's vibrant markets for an authentic experience. Farmers' markets are a riot of colors and aromas, showcasing fresh produce, artisanal cheeses, and regional delicacies. Engage with passionate vendors and learn about the raw ingredients that underpin Traditional Strasbourg Cuisine.

6. Indulge in Foie Gras: No trip to Alsace is complete without indulging in the decadent delight that is foie gras. This culinary treasure, prepared with meticulous care, exemplifies the region's commitment to gastronomic

excellence. It goes perfectly with a glass of local Gewürztraminer wine.

7. Kouglof, a traditional Alsatian cake, is a sweet way to end your culinary journey. This ring-shaped treat, adorned with almonds and dusted with powdered sugar, exemplifies the region's baking prowess. It pairs well with a cup of aromatic coffee from one of Strasbourg's charming cafes.

8. Wine Culture: Alsace is known for producing high-quality wines, and Strasbourg is no exception. Explore the city's wine bars and enjoy the crispness of a Riesling or the fruity notes of a Pinot Gris. Engage in discussions with local vintners who are enthusiastic about sharing their knowledge and showcasing the region's diverse terroir.

9. Festive Traditions: If you visit during one of Strasbourg's many festivals, you're in for a treat. Christmas markets, in particular, provide a sensory overload of scents and sights. Indulge in seasonal treats such as bredele (Christmas cookies) and vin chaud (mulled wine), and immerse yourself in the city's festive atmosphere.

Finally, Traditional Strasbourg Cuisine is a cultural experience that invites you to savor the history, traditions, and warmth of this enthralling region. Allow your taste buds to guide you through a culinary journey that captures the essence of Strasbourg's gastronomic soul as you navigate the cobblestone streets and timber-framed houses.

Preparation Tips

Cooking Traditional Strasbourg Cuisine in your own kitchen is a delightful culinary adventure that promises to bring the flavors of Alsace to your table. We'll show you how to make two classic dishes: tarte flambée and baeckeoffe.

Tarte Flambée: Flatbread or pizza dough
1 cup cream of tartar
100g bacon, thinly sliced 1 large onion, thinly sliced
season with salt and pepper to taste
Instructions:

Preheat your oven to its highest temperature (typically 475°F or 245°C).

Flatten the flatbread or roll out the pizza dough on a baking sheet.

Spread crème fraîche generously over the dough, leaving a small border around the edges.

Spread the crème fraîche evenly with thinly sliced onions and bacon.

To taste, season with salt and pepper.

Bake for 10-15 minutes, or until the edges are golden and the toppings are cooked in a preheated oven.

Remove from the oven and set aside for a few minutes before slicing and serving.

Ingredients for Baeckeoffe

500g beef, lamb, and pork cubed, 3 large potatoes peeled and sliced, 2 onions peeled and sliced, 2 carrots thinly sliced, 1 leek sliced, 2 garlic cloves sliced, 2 bay leaves minced

1 tsp thyme

season with salt and pepper to taste

1 1/2 cup white wine, dry

1 1/2 cups broth, either beef or vegetable

Instructions:

Preheat your oven to 350 degrees Fahrenheit (175 degrees Celsius).

Marinate the cubed meats with salt, pepper, and minced garlic in a large mixing bowl. Allow at least 30 minutes for it to sit.

Layer the sliced potatoes, onions, carrots, and leek in a large heavy-bottomed pot.

Arrange the marinated meat over the vegetables.

Among the layers, tuck bay leaves and thyme sprigs.

Pour in enough white wine to cover the ingredients.

Place the covered pot in the preheated oven. Bake the meat for 2.5 to 3 hours, or until tender.

When the Baeckeoffe is done, serve it hot and enjoy the rich, flavorful stew.

To enhance your dining experience, pair these dishes with a crisp Alsace Riesling or Gewürztraminer. As you savor each bite, you'll be transported to Strasbourg's picturesque streets, reveling in the authenticity of Traditional Strasbourg Cuisine. Good luck!

Strasbourg Top 10 Best Restaurants

Your taste buds are in for a whirlwind romance, from hearty Alsatian feasts to avant-garde artistry on plates. Buckle up for a delectable journey through Strasbourg's top ten restaurants, sure to tantalize your palate and leave you with memories richer than Alsatian flammekueche.

1. Gurtler Haut-Koenig: Ascend to the opulent Rohan Palace for a gastronomic paradise. Gurtler Haut-Koenig, a two-star Michelin restaurant, creates flavor symphonies using locally sourced, seasonal ingredients. Consider melt-in-your-mouth foie gras topped with caramelized apples, or tender turbot encased in a delicate Champagne sauce. Every bite is a poem written by chef Mathieu Beck, his passion dripping like vibrant watercolor onto the pristine plates.

2. Au Crocodile: At Au Crocodile, expect an Alsatian fairytale. This Michelin-starred gem, nestled in a half-timbered house, serves hearty, time-honored dishes like grandmotherly coq au vin and choucroute garnie piled high with plump sausages and tangy sauerkraut. The atmosphere is welcoming and warm, with exposed beams and flickering candles telling stories of bygone feasts.

3. Le Tire-Bouchon: Look no further than Le Tire-Bouchon for an authentic taste of Strasbourg's soul. The joyous chatter of locals draws them in, drawn in by the generous portions and unpretentious charm. Sink your teeth into an Alsatian pizza, flammekueche, with its paper-thin crust crackling beneath a symphony of caramelized onions, smoky bacon, and creamy Munster cheese. Allow it to flow with a hearty sip of local Gewurztraminer.

4. La Maison Kammerzell: La Maison Kammerzell transports you to a medieval wonderland. This historic landmark, adorned with whimsical carvings and stained glass windows, transports you to a time of chivalry and banquets. Baeckeoffe, a fragrant stew of meat and potatoes, or onglet de veau, tender veal bathed in a rich mushroom sauce, are two Alsatian specialties to try. Each dish is a delectable tribute to Strasbourg's illustrious culinary history.

5. Le Bistanquet: Looking for a contemporary spin on Alsatian classics? Your playground is the Bistanquet. Chef Adrien Weber reimagines regional flavors with playful irreverence, plating

dishes such as duck breast lacquered with cherry gastrique and foie gras ravioli dancing in a saffron broth. The setting is sleek and modern, the ideal complement to the vibrant tapestry of flavors on your plate.

6. Les Secrets d'une Grand-Mère: Les Secrets d'une Grand-Mère takes you deep into the heart of Alsatian home cooking. The aroma of simmering stews and freshly baked bread wafting through the air like a siren song at this family-run restaurant. Enjoy the richness of coq au Riesling or the buttery goodness of a Kugelhopf, a traditional Alsatian brioche. It's a culinary hug in a bowl, topped with a heaping spoonful of grandma's love.

7. Chez Yvonne: At Chez Yvonne, you can experience the vibrant pulse of Strasbourg's Petite France district. This vibrant brasserie is a

kaleidoscope of color and energy, the air alive with the clinking of glasses and animated conversation. Consume a succulent onglet de boeuf or share a massive flammekueche with friends while soaking up the infectious joie de vivre. It's a feast for the senses, one bite at a time.

8. Maison Alsacienne: If you want a taste of Strasbourg's grand dame elegance, go to Maison Alsacienne. This historic mansion exudes refined sophistication as it is bathed in soft lamplight. The menu is a tapestry of Alsatian grandeur, with delicate pike quenelles in beurre blanc and venison medallions garnished with a tart cranberry sauce. It's a memorable fine-dining experience.

9. Le Stras' 689: Do you want to experience the global village without leaving Strasbourg? The

689 at Le Stras is your passport to culinary adventures. Menu items include Thai green curry chicken, Moroccan tagines, and juicy American steaks. It's a culinary celebration with a side of Strasbourg's trademark warmth.

Chapter 4: Top 10 Outdoor Activities

Strasbourg has something for everyone, from peaceful cruises on the Il River to exciting bike excursions through rolling vineyards. So put on your walking shoes, grab your adventurous spirit, and get ready to discover the best 10 outdoor activities that will make your Strasbourg holiday unforgettable:

1. Take a lovely boat cruise down the Ill River, seeing half-timbered houses, charming bridges, and picturesque canals. Imagine yourself floating through a Renaissance painting as you pass beneath the Petite France neighborhood, a UNESCO World Heritage Site, and marvel at the unique covered bridges decked with flowers. Don't forget to wave to the sunbathers lounging on the riverbanks or the kayakers paddling nearby.

2. Pedal Through Vineyards: Explore the Alsace wine region on two wheels. Rent a bike and ride the Véloroute du Canal de la Bruche, a 74-kilometer road that winds through lovely villages, golden vineyards, and lush meadows. Stop for a picnic lunch amidst the rolling hills, sip a glass of Riesling at a nearby winery, and take in the spectacular views. This leisurely ride is ideal for families and those wanting a peaceful vacation.

3. Climb the Petite Venise: Get your heart beating by climbing to the top of the Barrage Vauban, a 17th-century dam with panoramic views of the city. Hike into the Petite Venise, a hidden paradise lying behind the dam, and discover waterfalls, grottoes, and rich flora. The prize? Views of Strasbourg's spires, the Ill River flowing through the city, and the Vosges Mountains in the background.

4. Picnic in Parc de l'Orangerie: Bring a baguette, some local cheese, and a bottle of wine to the expansive Parc de l'Orangerie, a paradise for leisure and amusement. Rent a boat and paddle around the lake, take a stroll through the rose garden, or simply relax under a tree and soak up the sun. Don't miss the Orangery, a spectacular 18th-century building that today houses exhibitions and performances.

5. Kayak on the Ill River: Kayak on the Ill River to see Strasbourg from a different perspective. Paddle along the canals, pass beneath bridges, and appreciate the city's architectural beauties from the water's edge. Kayaking tours are accessible at all skill levels, making it a fun pastime for couples, families, and lone visitors alike.

6. Wander through the cobblestone alleyways of Petite France, a district right out of a fantasy. Admire the flower-adorned half-timbered cottages, photograph the gorgeous canals, and visit the small stores selling local crafts and gifts. Don't miss the Maison Kammerzell, a 15th-century timber-framed building considered one of Strasbourg's architectural beauties.

7. Ascend the 332 steps to the top of Strasbourg Cathedral for a bird's-eye perspective of the city. Admire the elaborate gargoyles, gaze through the sunlight-bathed stained-glass windows, and take in the panoramic view of the city. On a clear day, you might even see the Black Forest in the distance.

8. Cycle Through Strasbourg: Rent a bike and experience Strasbourg's large network of cycling trails. Pass via Notre Dame Cathedral and Place Gutenberg on your way to the Petite Venise for a calm getaway. You can even take a longer trip along the Canal de la Marne au Rhin, taking in the fresh air and magnificent vistas.

9. Visit the Christmas Markets: If you're visiting during the holiday season, immerse yourself in the beauty of Strasbourg's Christmas markets. Sip hot mulled wine, eat gingerbread cookies, and shop kiosks brimming with handcrafted decorations and locally made goods. From Place Gutenberg to Petite France, the entire city is transformed into a winter wonderland of festive pleasure.

10. Explore the Natural Beauty Surrounding Strasbourg: Go beyond the city core and explore the natural beauty that surrounds Strasbourg. Hike through the Vosges Mountains, kayak along the Rhine, or visit the Parc Naturel Régional des Vosges du Nord. These trips provide an opportunity to get some fresh air, reconnect with nature, and explore picturesque communities and hidden jewels.

Strasbourg's outdoor activities are as varied as its history and culture. Whether you're looking for adrenaline-pumping adventures, quiet excursions, or romantic strolls, the city provides something for everyone.

Top Attractions

In this Subchapter , we'll look at some of the greatest sights in Strasbourg that are sure to captivate any tourist.

1. Strasbourg Cathedral

A journey to Strasbourg would be incomplete without a visit to the renowned Strasbourg

Cathedral. This Gothic masterpiece, also known as Notre-Dame de Strasbourg, is one of Europe's most stunning cathedrals and a must-see site for anybody visiting the city. The cathedral's ornate front has gorgeous sculptures and carvings, while its interior features beautiful stained glass windows and an amazing organ. Visitors can climb to the top of the cathedral's tower for panoramic views of the city.

2. Petite France : Petite France is a lovely area in Strasbourg notable for its attractive canals, half-timbered buildings, and cobblestone lanes. This region was previously home to tanners, millers, and fishermen, but it is now a famous tourist destination with a variety of stores, restaurants, and cafes. Visitors can enjoy a leisurely stroll along the canals or a relaxing boat cruise to appreciate the splendor of this ancient area.

3. Palais Rohan : The Palais Rohan is a spectacular 18th-century palace that today houses three museums: the Museum of Decorative Arts, the Museum of Fine Arts, and the Archaeological Museum. The magnificent interiors of the palace offer finely adorned rooms and halls that provide an insight into the lives of the aristocracy during the 18th century. The museums house a remarkable collection of paintings, furniture, and decorative pieces that are likely to please any art lover.

4. Parc de l'Orangerie

The Parc de l'Orangerie is a lovely park in Strasbourg, ideal for a pleasant afternoon stroll or a picnic. This sprawling park contains lush foliage, a lake, and a zoo with over 120 animal species. Visitors can also ride the park's mini-train or rent a boat to explore the lake.

5. La Petite France Christmas Market : If you're in Strasbourg over the holidays, don't miss out on the La Petite France Christmas Market. This market is one of Europe's oldest and largest Christmas markets, with over 300 stalls selling everything from handmade presents to traditional Alsatian cuisine and drink. The market is hosted in the heart of Petite France and is a magical experience that should not be missed.

Musee Alsacien : The Musee Alsacien is an intriguing museum that highlights the history and culture of the Alsace area. The museum's collection contains traditional clothing, furniture, tools, and domestic artifacts that provide insight into daily life in Alsace during the 18th and 19th centuries. Visitors can also learn about the region's cultures and traditions through interactive exhibitions and displays.

7. Vauban's Barrage

The Barrage Vauban is a historic dam and bridge erected in the 17th century to defend the city from flooding. Today, the Barrage Vauban is a renowned tourist destination that provides breathtaking views of the city and its surrounds. Visitors can climb to the top of the dam for panoramic views of Strasbourg's cityscape or take a leisurely stroll along the bridge to enjoy the river's splendor.

8. Rohan Palace Gardens : The Rohan Palace Gardens are a charming sanctuary in the center of Strasbourg, ideal for a tranquil afternoon stroll. These gardens have nicely kept lawns, fountains, and a variety of plants and flowers. Visitors can also tour the palace's courtyard and observe its spectacular architecture.

9th. Strasbourg Museum of Modern and Contemporary Art : The Strasbourg Museum of Modern and Contemporary Art is a must-see for art aficionados. This museum displays an amazing collection of modern and contemporary art ranging from the nineteenth century to the present day. The museum's collection includes works by well-known painters such as Pablo Picasso, Joan Miró, and Wassily Kandinsky.

10th. Strasbourg Christmas Market : The Strasbourg Christmas Market is one of Europe's oldest and most prominent Christmas markets.

This market has approximately 300 stalls selling anything from handmade souvenirs to traditional Alsatian food and drink. Visitors can also enjoy festive music, entertainment, and activities throughout the market.

10 Important Safety Tips

Strasbourg, like any other tourist location, has its own set of safety problems that visitors should be aware of. This post will look at ten crucial safety precautions for people visiting Strasbourg.

1. Be on the lookout for pickpockets.

Pickpockets are common in Strasbourg, as they are in any big tourist destination. These thieves frequently prey on people in busy places such as train stations, markets, and tourist attractions. Keep your valuables close to your body and stay alert of your surroundings to prevent being a victim of pickpocketing. Carrying big quantities of cash or wearing expensive jewelry in public is not recommended.

2. At night, remain in well-lit locations.

While Strasbourg is a typically safe city, staying in well-lit places at night is always a smart idea. Avoid wandering alone in dark or remote regions, especially if the area is unfamiliar to you. Stick to well-traveled routes, and if you're out late, consider taking a cab or public transportation.

3. Exercise extreme caution when utilizing ATMs.

ATM skimming is a widespread problem in Strasbourg and other major tourist sites. These crooks capture your credit card details and PIN number using covert cameras and equipment. Use ATMs within banks or other secure locations to prevent being a victim of ATM skimming. When entering your PIN, cover the keyboard and be aware of anyone who appears to be monitoring you.

4. Keep an eye out for oncoming vehicles.

Strasbourg is a busy city with a lot of traffic, therefore crossing the street should be done with caution. Always utilize marked crosswalks and keep an eye out for oncoming vehicles. Even if the light is green, always look both ways before crossing. When walking near traffic, avoid using your phone or other distractions.

5. Use caution in congested locations.

Markets, festivals, and tourist destinations that are overcrowded can be targets for terrorism or other violent activities. keep mindful of your surroundings and report any suspicious activity to authorities to keep safe in these regions. To avoid becoming a target for thieves, carry a small bag or backpack that you can keep close to your body.

Maintain the security of your passport and other critical documents.

Your passport and other critical documents are valuable objects that should always be kept safe. Consider carrying a copy of your passport instead of the original, and storing it securely, such as in a hotel safe. Anyone who requests to view your passport or other documentation, especially if they are not in uniform, should be avoided.

7. Take advantage of trusted cab services.

If you need to take a cab in Strasbourg, make sure to choose with a trustworthy company.

Look for certified taxi stands or ask your hotel for a reputable service recommendation. Take unmarked cabs or accept rides from strangers as they can be unsafe and lead to theft or other crimes.

8. Use public transit with caution.

Although public transportation in Strasbourg is generally safe, it is vital to exercise caution when taking buses or trains. Maintain vigilance over your valuables and be mindful of your surroundings. Avoid traveling late at night alone and instead consider using a taxi.

9. Study some fundamental French phrases.

Although many people in Strasbourg understand English, it's always a good idea to learn a few basic French words before you travel. This will allow you to communicate with locals and ask for assistance if necessary. Consider studying "Bonjour" (hello), "Merci" (thank you), and "Où est la gare?" (Where is the train station?).

10. Keep up with local news and events.

Finally, while in Strasbourg, it is critical to stay up to date on local events and news. This will help you avoid any potential safety hazards and will make navigating the city easier. Consider downloading a local news app or visiting local news websites for the most up-to-date information on current events and safety concerns.

Chapter 5: Culture and History

Strasbourg is a city rich in history and culture, making it a must-see for any traveler. Strasbourg, located in northeastern France, has a distinct blend of French and German influences, which can be seen in its architecture, cuisine, and language.

History

Strasbourg's history may be traced back to the Roman era, when it was known as Argentoratum. It was an important trade and commercial center, as well as a military station. Strasbourg became a prominent textile manufacturing base in the Middle Ages, producing beautiful linen and silk.

Strasbourg became a hub for humanism and learning during the Renaissance period, with many renowned professors and intellectuals residing there. The city was particularly significant in the Protestant Reformation, with Martin Luther visiting in 1518.

Strasbourg has recently been at the focus of European politics and diplomacy. It is the home of the European Parliament, which meets in the city's modernist glass edifice, and has played a significant role in defining Europe's destiny.

Culture

Strasbourg's culture is a combination of both French and German elements. Alsatian, a blend of French and German, is the city's dialect.

Strasbourg's Christmas markets, which attract millions of people each year, are one of the city's most recognizable cultural icons. The markets, which take place around the city, provide a variety of traditional Alsatian delicacies and goods. Visitors can try local delicacies like mulled wine, gingerbread, and sausages while perusing shops selling handmade ornaments and gifts.

The architecture of Strasbourg is another essential component of its culture. The historic heart of the city, known as Grande Île, is a UNESCO World Heritage Site and home to some of Europe's best examples of Gothic and Renaissance architecture. The Cathedral of

Notre-Dame, which dates back to the 12th century and contains spectacular stained glass windows and complex woodwork, is the city's most recognizable structure.

Food is an essential aspect of Strasbourg culture, with a variety of regional specialties to try. The tarte flambée, a thin-crust pizza-like delicacy topped with cream, onions, and bacon, is famous in the city. Choucroute, a substantial dish of sauerkraut and pork, and baeckeoffe, a slow-cooked casserole of meat and potatoes, are two more regional favorites.

- *National Gallery*

I couldn't help but feel a sense of exhilaration and anticipation as I walked through the streets of Strasbourg. I was on my way to the National Gallery of Strasbourg, one of France's most important art institutions.

As an art enthusiast, I had been anticipating this visit for weeks. I'd heard great things about the museum's remarkable collection of paintings and sculptures, and I couldn't wait to see them for myself.

The majesty and splendor of the museum struck me as I approached it. With its exquisite façade and numerous embellishments, the building was a piece of art in and of itself. I couldn't wait to see what was on the inside.

I was greeted by a polite staff member who gave me a map of the galleries as soon as I entered the museum. The museum was separated into parts, each of which was dedicated to a distinct period or style of art.

My journey began in the Renaissance section, which contained paintings by some of the period's most famous artists, including Leonardo da Vinci and Raphael. With their vibrant colors and precise workmanship, the artworks were breathtakingly gorgeous. I felt like I'd been transported to another age.

Then I went to the Baroque section, which featured masterpieces by Caravaggio and Rubens. I was captivated by the power and intensity of the paintings in this part, which were distinguished by their dramatic lighting and deep emotions.

I was astounded by the sheer range of art on show as I made my way through the museum. There was something for everyone to enjoy, ranging from ancient sculptures to contemporary installations.

The Impressionist art collection at the museum was one of the highlights of my tour. With their vivid hues and exquisite brushstrokes, the works of artists such as Monet and Renoir were simply magnificent. I could have spent hours marveling at these works of art.

Another noteworthy area of the museum was the modern art gallery, which displayed works by some of the twentieth century's most innovative and important artists. I was intrigued to the abstract paintings and sculptures because they were thought-provoking and difficult.

The museum's commitment to displaying a varied spectrum of art and artists hit me throughout my stay. There was something for everyone, from the classics to the avant-garde.

I couldn't help but feel grateful as I exited the museum. In every sense, the National Gallery of Strasbourg exceeded my expectations, and I felt blessed to have had the opportunity to study its wonderful collection of art.

The National Gallery is a must-see for every art fan visiting Strasbourg. It is a true treasure of the city's cultural scene, with its outstanding collection of paintings and sculptures spanning centuries of artistic history.

Whether you are an experienced art collector or simply appreciate beauty and creativity, the National Gallery of Strasbourg is bound to inspire and enchant you. So why not schedule a visit today and see for yourself the delights of this magnificent museum?

- *The Strasbourg Museum*

The Strasbourg Museum, officially known as the Musée des Beaux-Arts de Strasbourg, is a must-see for art and history aficionados both. This museum, located in the center of Strasbourg, France, houses an outstanding collection of art and artifacts spanning centuries of artistic history.

The museum is housed in a stunning 18th-century edifice that was originally a bishop's palace in Strasbourg. The architecture of the building is worth admiring on its own, with its grand façade and intricate details. But it's what's on the inside that truly distinguishes this museum.

The collection at the Strasbourg Museum is vast and diverse, containing works by some of history's greatest artists. Visitors can expect to see paintings, sculptures, and other forms of art dating from the Renaissance period to the present.

One of the museum's highlights is its impressive collection of European art from the 14th to the 19th centuries. Visitors can admire works by artists such as Botticelli, Rubens, and Goya, among others. The paintings are beautifully displayed in spacious galleries that allow visitors to appreciate the details and intricacies of each piece.

The museum's collection of decorative arts is also noteworthy. This includes ceramics, glassware, furniture, and other objects that showcase the craftsmanship and artistry of their creators. Visitors can see examples of Art Nouveau, Art Deco, and other popular styles throughout history.

The Strasbourg Museum also has a lot to offer those who are interested in contemporary art. The museum frequently hosts temporary exhibitions that feature the work of emerging artists from around the world. These exhibits are frequently thought-provoking and challenging, making them an excellent way to engage with contemporary art.

In addition to its impressive art collection, the Strasbourg Museum has a rich history that visitors can explore. Visitors can learn about the building's history through guided tours or by exploring the museum's informative displays.

Chapter 6: Well Structure 7 Days Itinerary Plan

Day 1: Arrival and Orientation

Take some time to get oriented in Strasbourg when you arrive. Check into your hotel and go for a walk around the city center. Visit Strasbourg Cathedral, a stunning Gothic masterpiece that dominates the city skyline. Take a stroll through Petite France, a charming neighborhood with charming half-timbered houses and scenic canals.

Day 2: Museums and Galleries

Begin your day with a visit to the Strasbourg Museum. Spend some time admiring the impressive collection of art and artifacts spanning centuries of artistic history. After that, visit the Museum of Modern and Contemporary Art, which features works by contemporary artists from around the world. In the evening, attend a performance at the Opéra national du Rhin, one of France's premier opera houses.

Day 3: Wine Tasting and Countryside Tour

Take a break from the city and head to the countryside for a day of wine tasting and sightseeing. The Alsace region is known for its excellent wines, and you can visit local vineyards for tastings and tours. Along the way, visit picturesque villages such as Riquewihr and Colmar, which are known for their charming architecture and colorful houses.

Day 4: Boat Tour and Historical Sites

Take a boat tour along the Ill River to see the city from a different angle. After that, visit the Palais Rohan, a grand palace that houses three museums: the Museum of Decorative Arts, the Museum of Fine Arts, and the Archaeological Museum. Explore the exhibits to learn about Strasbourg's history and culture.

Day 5: Day Trip to Germany

Strasbourg is close to the German border, making it easy to take a day trip across the Rhine River. Visit nearby cities such as Freiburg or Heidelberg, which have charming old town centers and historic landmarks. Alternatively, head to the Black Forest for a day of hiking and exploring the region's natural beauty.

Day 6: Food Tour and Market Visit

No trip to Strasbourg is complete without trying the local cuisine. Take a food tour to sample traditional Alsatian dishes like choucroute (sauerkraut with sausages) and tarte flambée (a thin-crust pizza-like dish). Visit local markets, such as the Marché de Noel, a Christmas market held in December, to sample local specialties and pick up souvenirs.

Day 7: Cycling Tour and Parks

Rent a bike and explore the city's parks and gardens. Begin at the Parc de l'Orangerie, a sprawling park with a lake, a zoo, and a mini-golf course. Then, proceed to the Jardin des Deux Rives, a park that straddles the French-German border. Enjoy the scenic views and fresh air before returning to the city center for a final evening of dining and entertainment.

Conclusion

As you near the end of this Strasbourg travel guide book, it's difficult not to feel nostalgic for the experiences you've had in this wonderful city. Strasbourg captures your heart and imprints your soul.

Strasbourg is a city steeped in history and culture, from the magnificent Gothic Cathedral to the charming Petite France neighborhood.

Its museums and galleries provide an insight into the region's artistic and intellectual life, while wine country and countryside tours provide a welcome break from the hustle and bustle of city life.

But it is the people who truly distinguish Strasbourg. From the moment you arrive, the warm and welcoming locals make you feel at home, and their hospitality and kindness leave a lasting impression. The food is delicious, the wine is excellent, and the atmosphere is friendly and upbeat.

Take a moment to reflect on your time in Strasbourg as you close this book. Remember what you saw, heard, and smelled. Remember who you met and the memories you created. And know that Strasbourg will always have a special place in your heart, no matter where you go in life.

Happy Vacation

Printed in Great Britain
by Amazon